SUPER SIGHT

written by JENNIFER WHITEHEAD
pictures by EMILY REYMANN

Copyright © 2024 Super Book Series LLC. All rights reserved.

WWW.SUPERBOOKSERIES.COM

All rights reserved. No part of this publication may be reproduced, stored in a retrieval system or transmitted, in any form or by any means, electronic, mechanical, photocopying, recording or otherwise, without the prior permission of the copyright holder.

ISBN 978-1-7368086-3-4

Dedicated to this beautiful generation of children we're raising.

A special thank you to Nora and Julie.

When I was just a baby
as tiny as can be,
my grown-ups began to wonder
if I might need help to see.

I tried to focus my eyes
to play with my favorite toy,
but things looked pretty fuzzy.
Playtime was hard to enjoy.

My doctor checked my focus,
eye health and eye movement.

This helped her understand
where I needed improvement.

When I started wearing glasses,
everything became so clear.
They helped me see like a superhero,
no matter how far or near.

Underneath my glasses
I wore a patch to the right.
This helped strengthen my left eye
to give me my best sight.

My adult carefully helps me place on my glasses and patch during the day. It's not safe for anyone else to touch. If you touch, they might not stay.

Please know my patch is only temporary,
just like a cast.
I still have two beautiful eyes,
they're working hard so my sight will last.

When it's time to remove my patch,
I place it on my chart.
This helps me see all of my hard work,
and makes a special piece of art.

Sometimes I need eye drops,
I feel nervous when I do.
But if I'm brave and patient,
I feel proud of myself when I'm through.

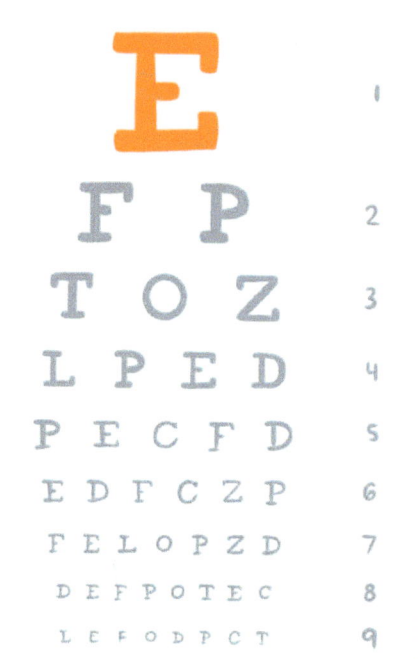

Each year I see my eye doctor.
She's gentle, kind and smart.
My eyes follow her small light,
then I name the letters on her chart.

Choosing new glasses is exciting,
I prefer them bold and bright.
I want to express my style as I grow,
I want something that feels just right.

There are many types of glasses,
I love to see each one.
Some are simple, some are fancy,
others protect you from the sun.

There is so much I want to see,
The colors fill me with delight.

When I wear my glasses,
Life looks and feels just right.

My glasses are a special part of my journey to be me.

I get to be my best self
when I can properly see.

We all have many superpowers.
I bet you're helpful, kind and bright.
Celebrating our special traits
fills us with love so we can shine our light.

www.ingramcontent.com/pod-product-compliance
Lightning Source LLC
LaVergne TN
LVHW071028070426
835507LV00002B/71